Norman Rockwell
PAINTS
AMERICA

by Carolyn Staven

Scott Foresman

Editorial Offices: Glenview, Illinois • New York, New York
Sales Offices: Reading, Massachusetts • Duluth, Georgia
Glenview, Illinois • Carrollton, Texas • Menlo Park, California

When librarians are asked for books about famous American artists, one person they may think of is Norman Rockwell. He probably painted more pictures of American life than any other artist.

Norman Rockwell was born in 1894, in New York City. He was one of two sons born to Nancy and Jarvis Rockwell. Norman Rockwell was tall and skinny, and he had a long neck. He looked awkward next to his brother, who was named Jarvis, after his father. Jarvis Rockwell was good at sports. Norman Rockwell was a dreamer. He was good at art and loved to draw.

**Norman Rockwell (back center)
with his family**

At bedtime, Rockwell's father read stories
to him and his brother. Rockwell imagined
what the people and places in the stories looked
like. Then he would draw them. Art was the
biggest part of Rockwell's life. He was drawing
all the time.

Rockwell's parents could see that he was talented. His father and grandfather had been good at art too. Every Saturday Rockwell went to the Chase School of Art. He learned to draw figures of people.

At age sixteen, Rockwell left high school. He really wanted to be an artist. He may have been a dreamer, but he knew he would have to work hard. He went to another art school to learn painting.

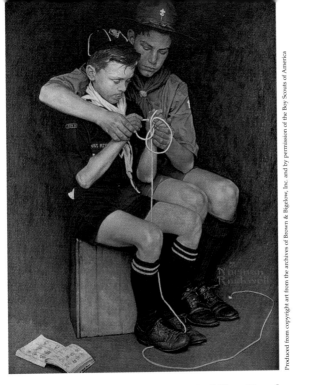

A Guiding Hand,
Boy Scout Calendar painting, 1946

Rockwell soon found a job. He did the art for Boy Scout calendars and hiking books. The Boy Scouts loved his work! He was put in charge of all the art for their magazine. It was called *Boys' Life.*

Rockwell's art appeared in *Boys' Life* and in other Boy Scout books and calendars for more than fifty years! These works of art were some of the best created in America at the time.

Rockwell's first cover for
***The Saturday Evening Post*, 1916**

When Rockwell was twenty-two, he did the art for the cover of a popular magazine. It was called *The Saturday Evening Post*. He didn't know it, but this would be the first of 320 covers Rockwell would draw and paint during the next forty years.

Now many more people saw Rockwell's artwork. He was still a young man. But he was already making a very good living doing what he loved.

Next Rockwell began to draw ads. His ads would make people smile, laugh, or feel warm inside. Then they would feel good about the product too.

One time he drew an ad for socks that had strong yarn in the toes and heels. They would last a long time. His ad showed a man with holes in all his clothes. But there were no holes in his socks! People saw what good socks these were. Many wanted to buy them.

Ad for Interwoven Socks, 1927

Freedom of Speech

When World War II began, Rockwell had an idea to paint four pictures. He hoped the pictures would help people remember the freedoms they were fighting for.

He called the illustrations *The Four Freedoms.* A town meeting showed *Freedom of Speech.* A Thanksgiving dinner showed *Freedom from Want.*